Stack

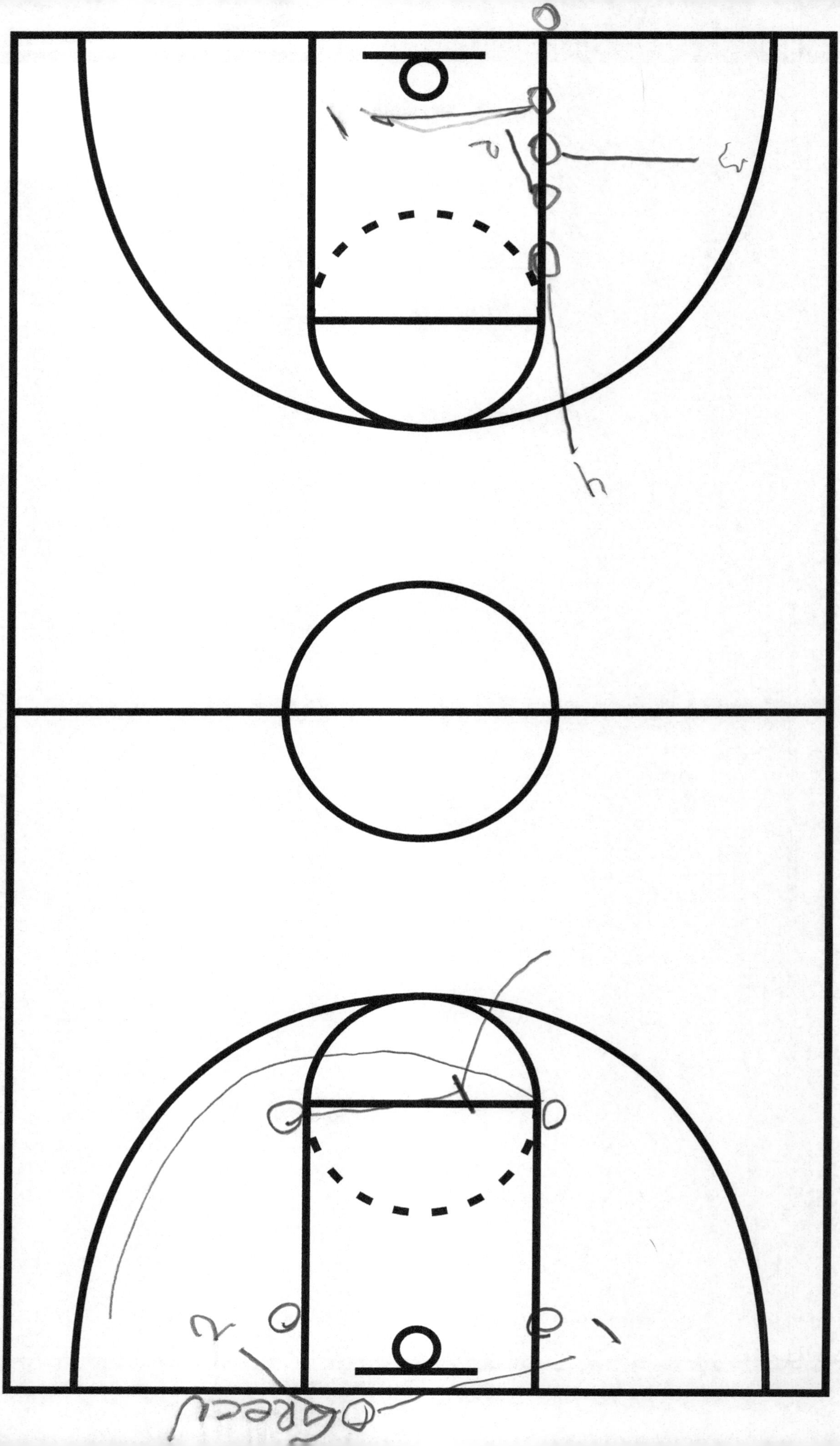

Slack

line

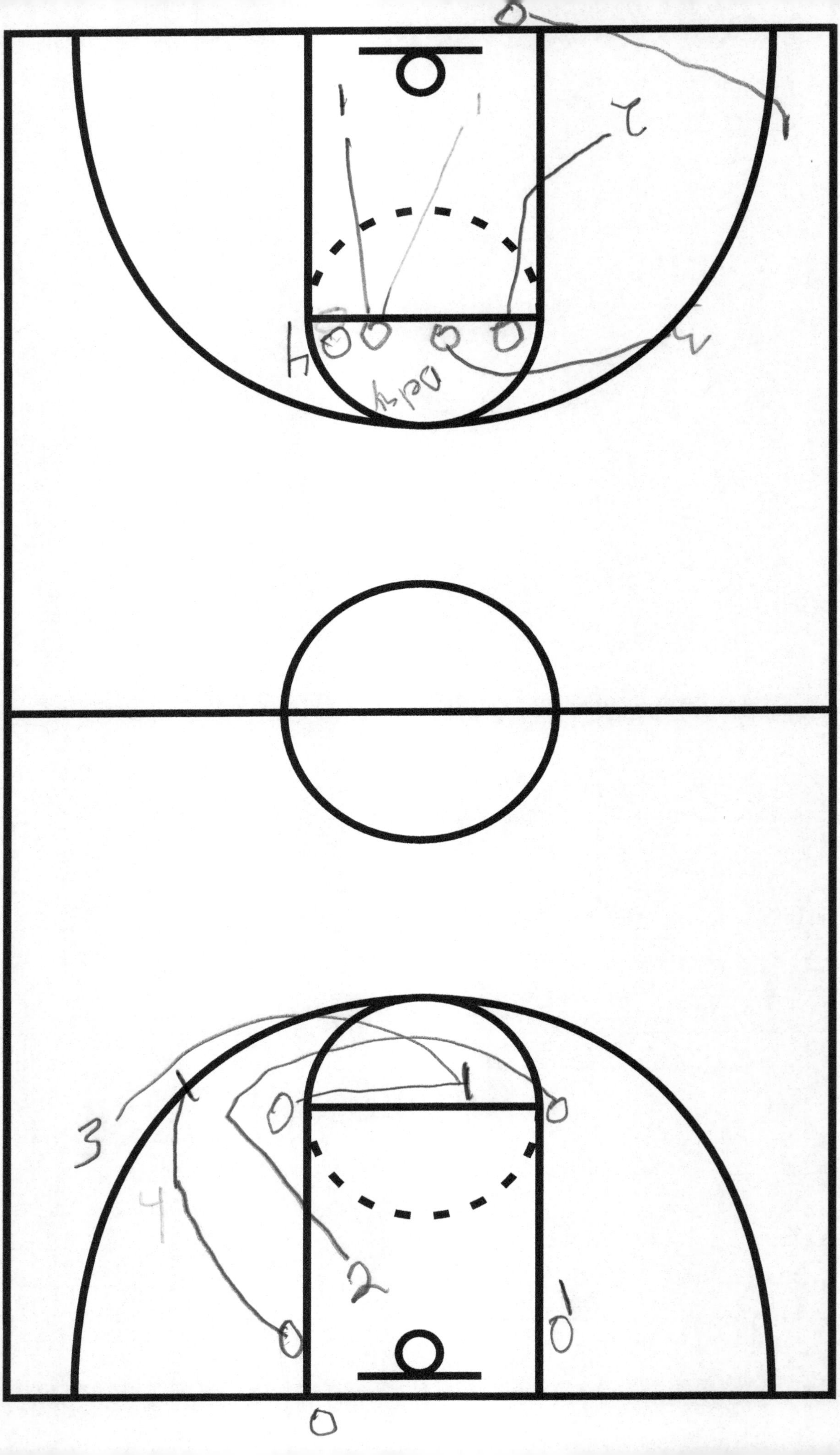

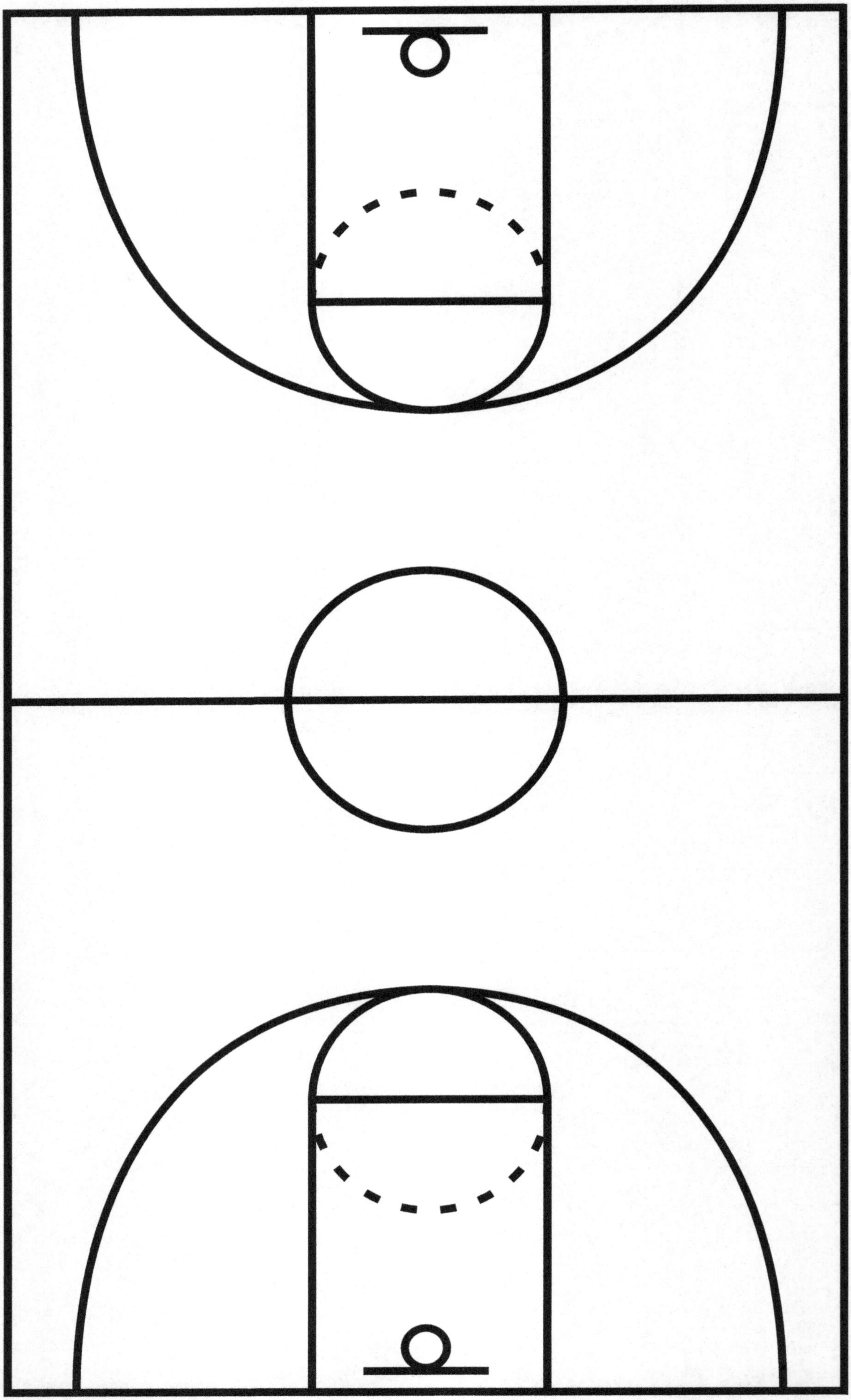

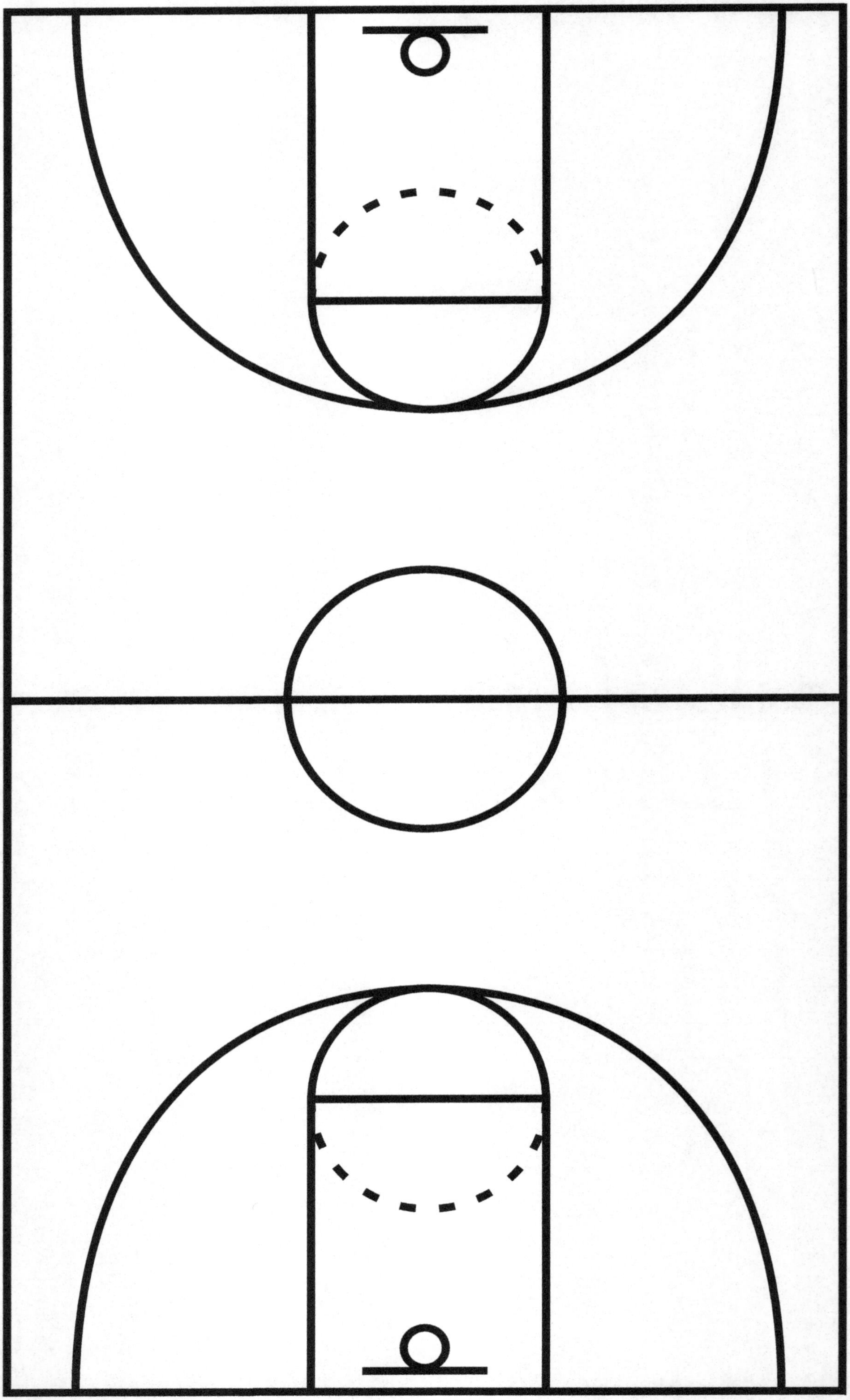

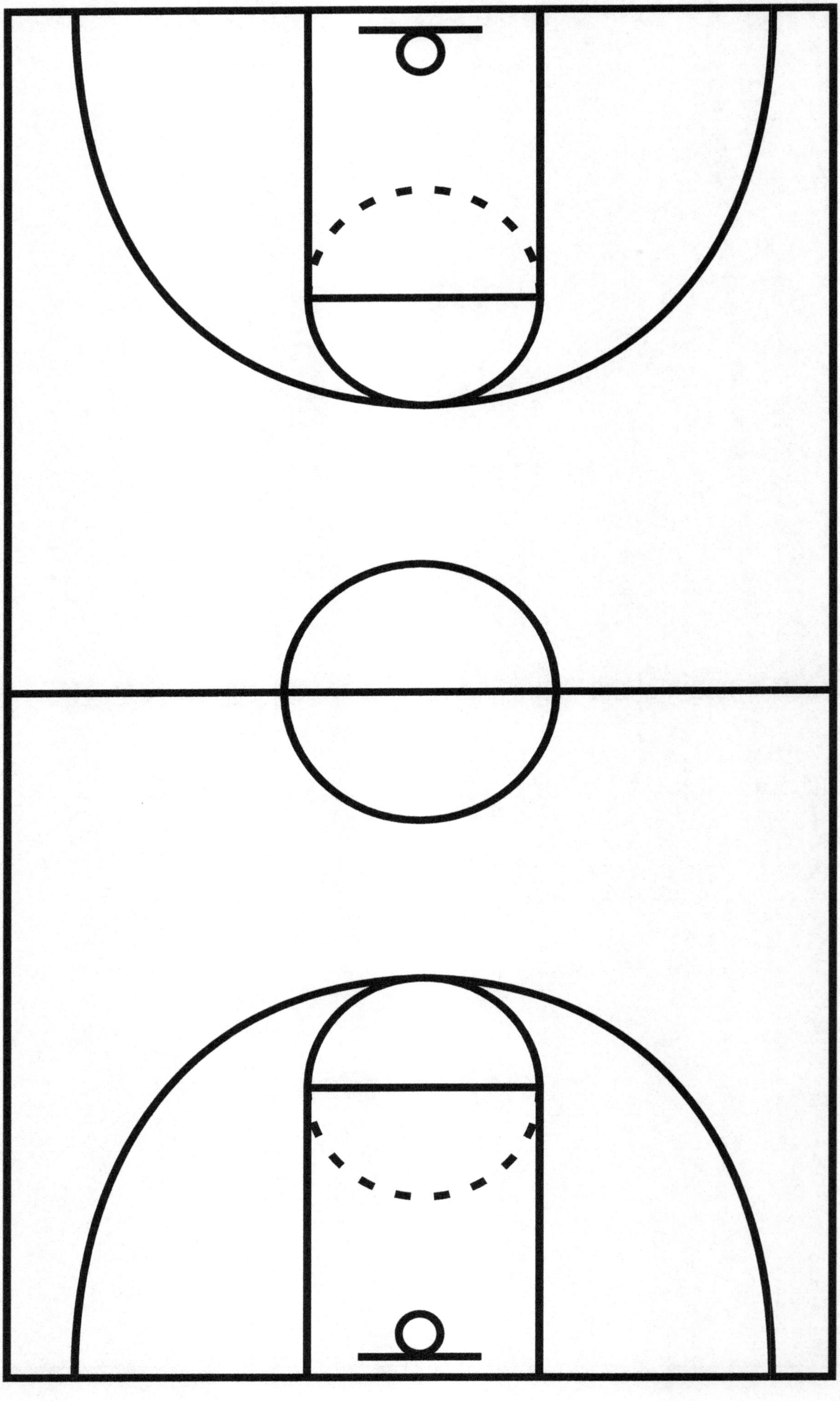

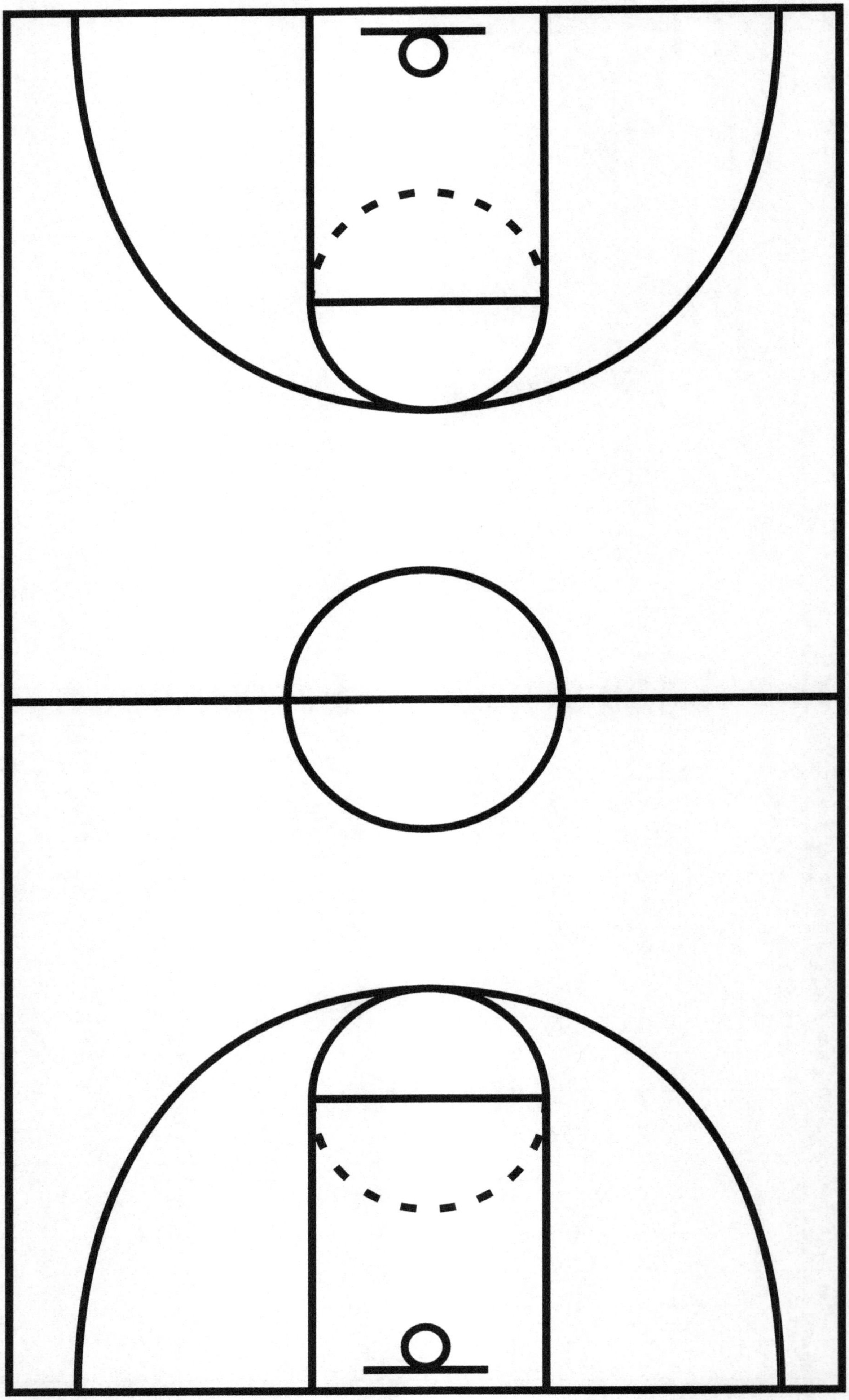

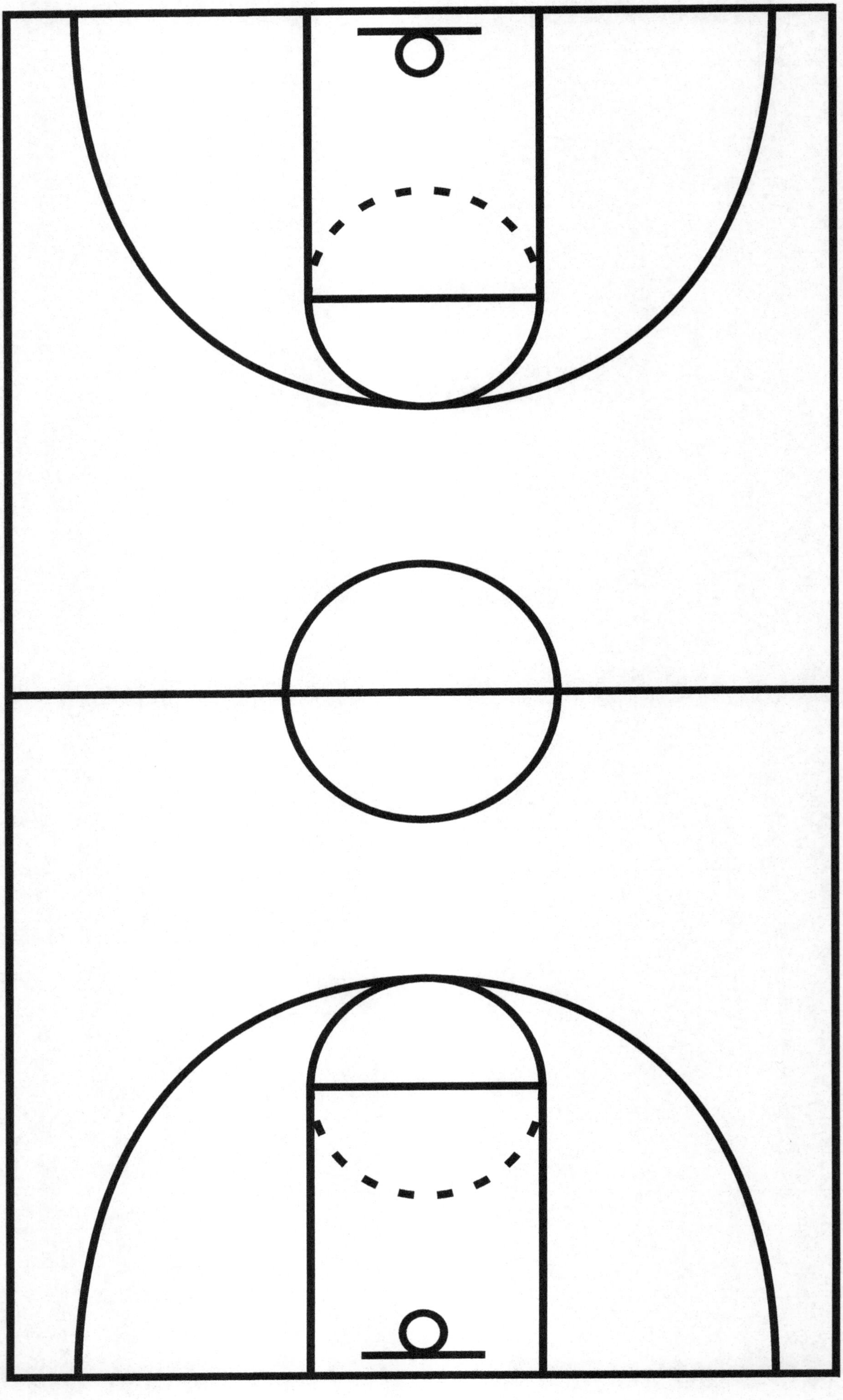

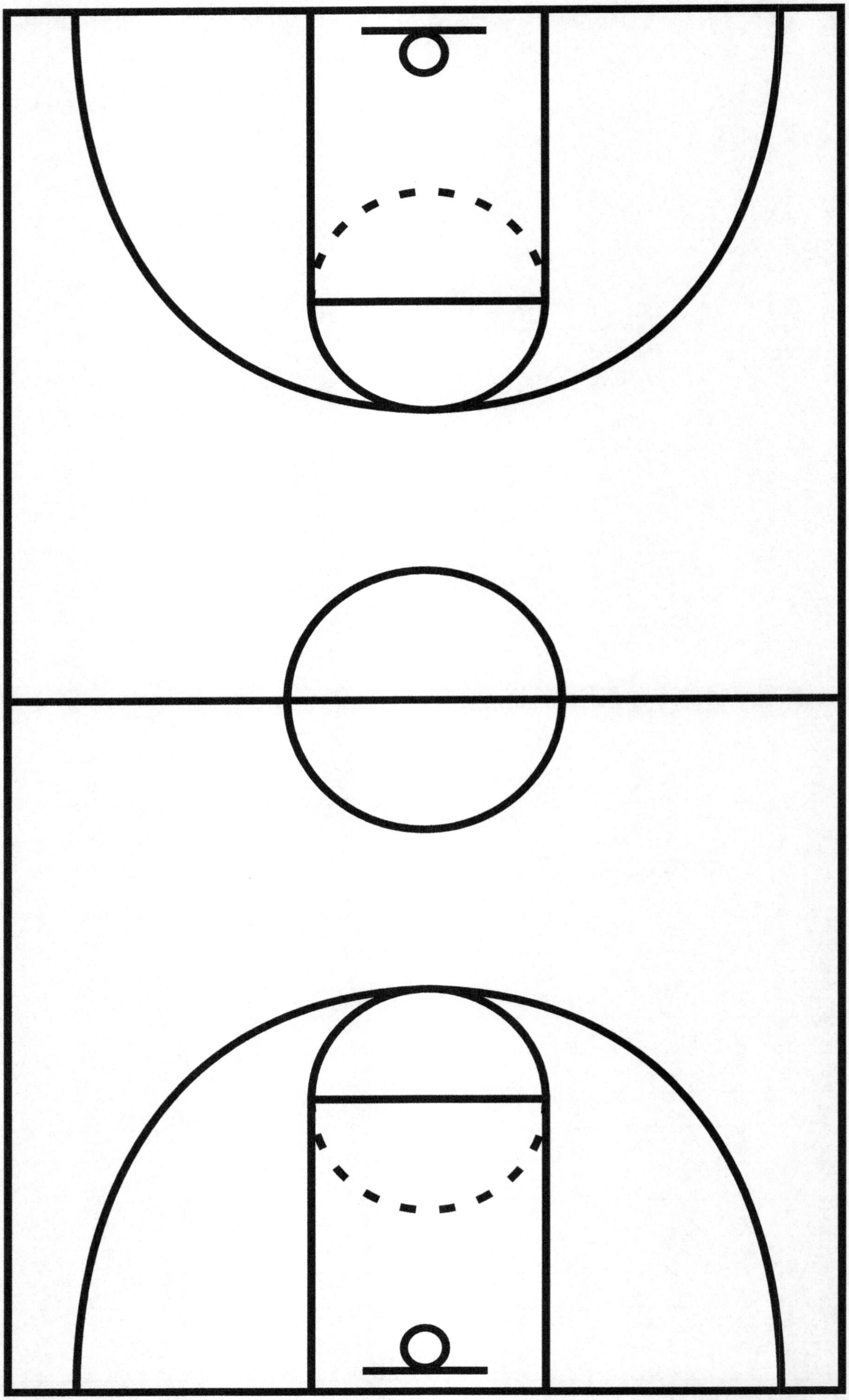

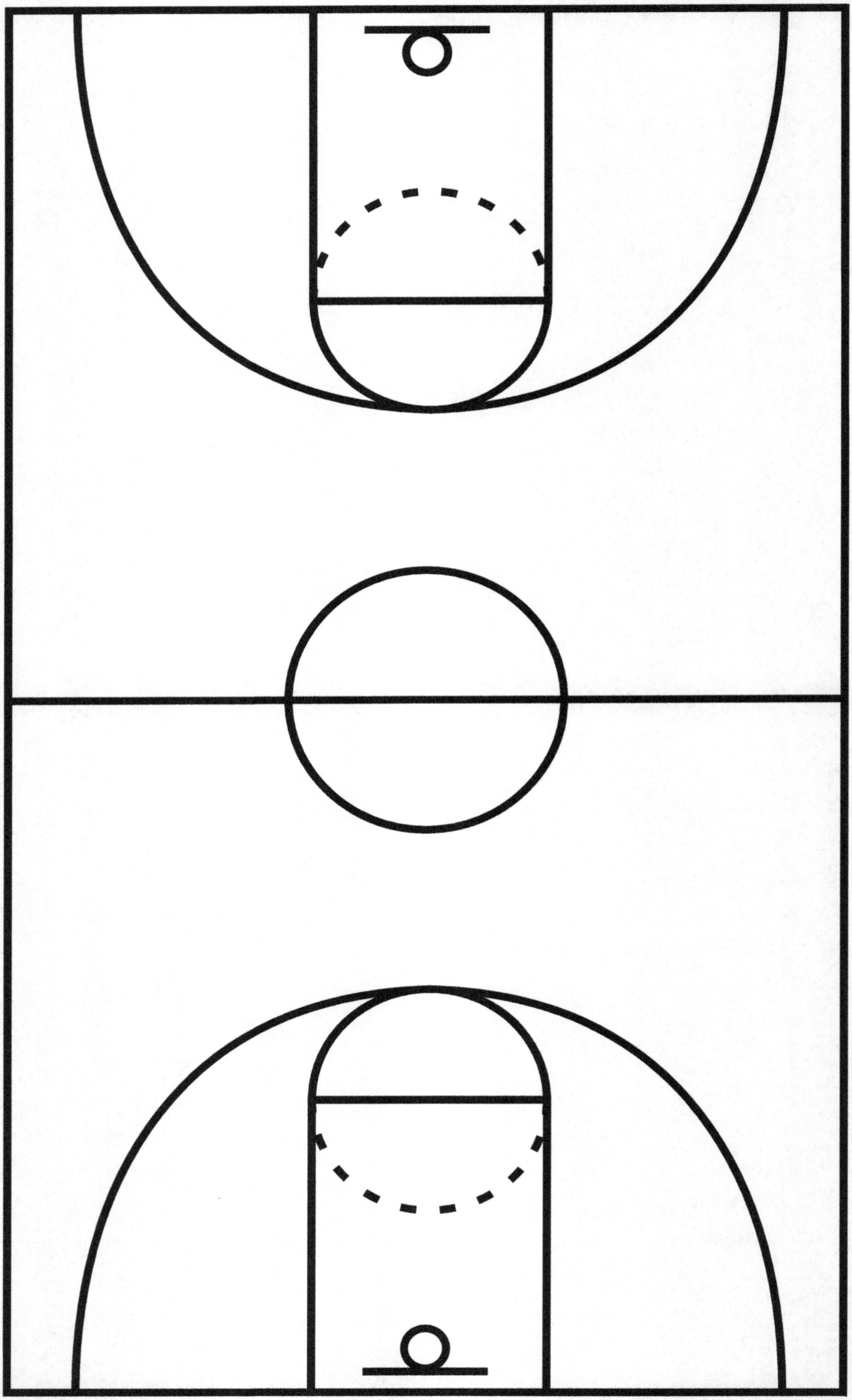

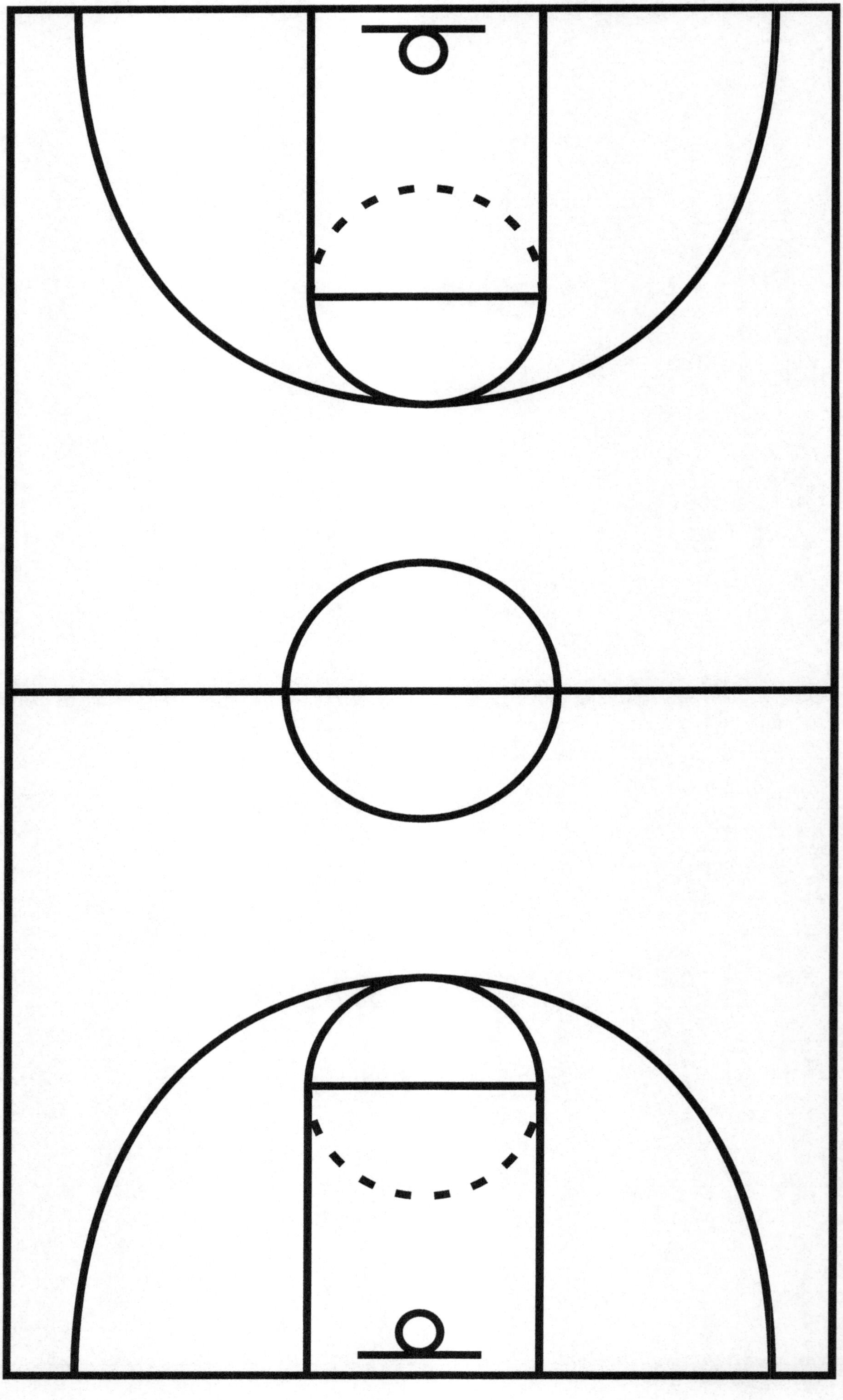

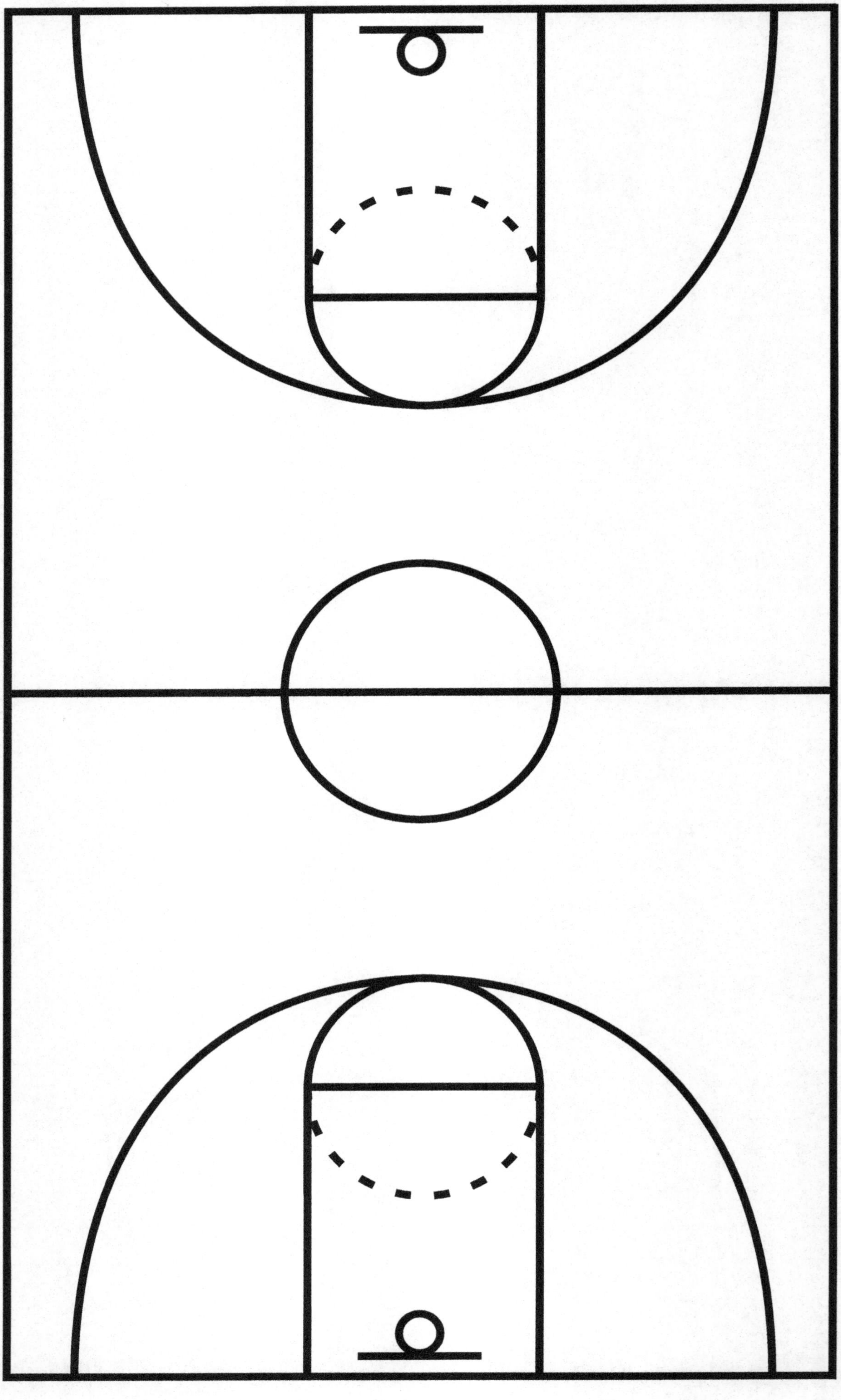

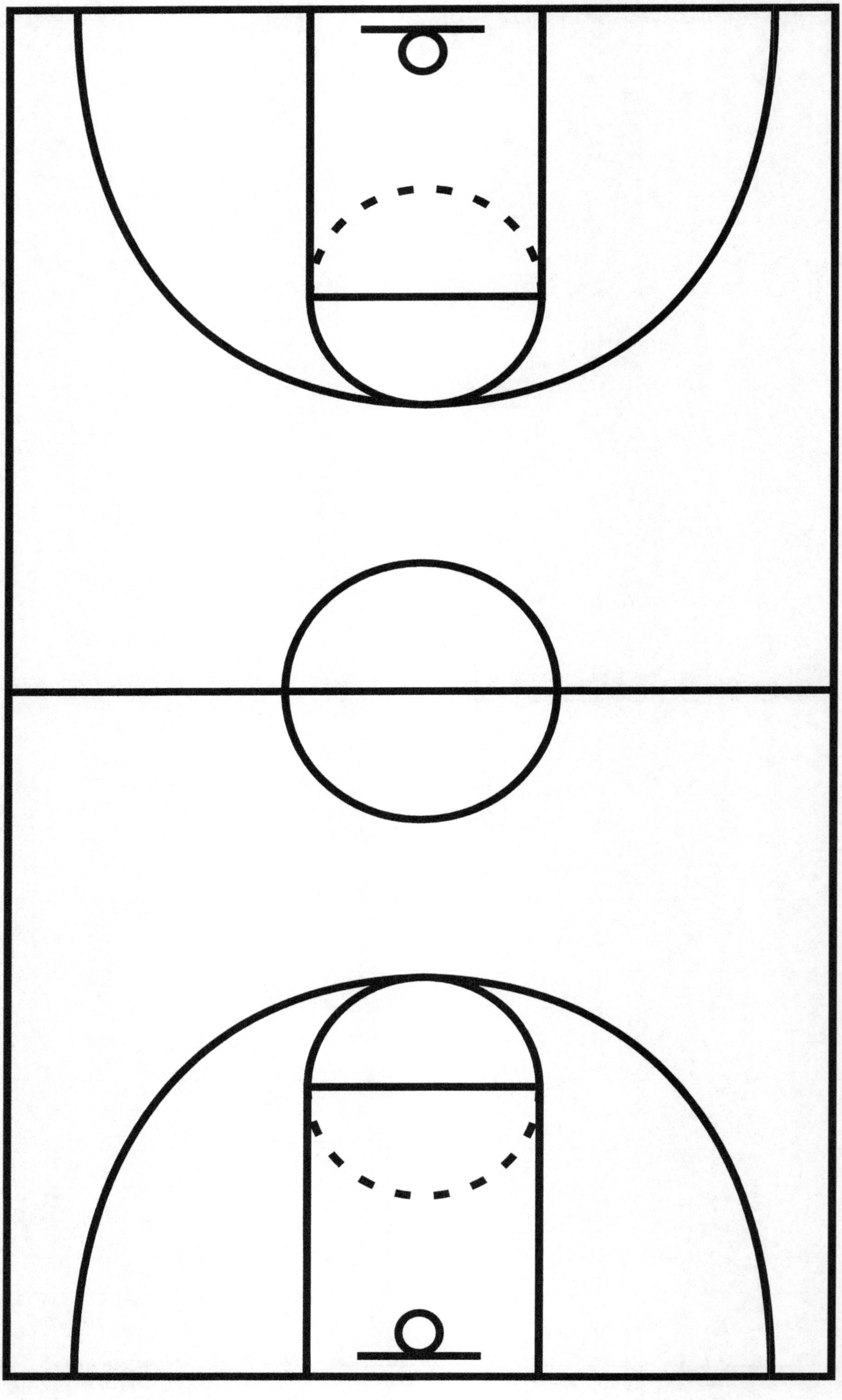

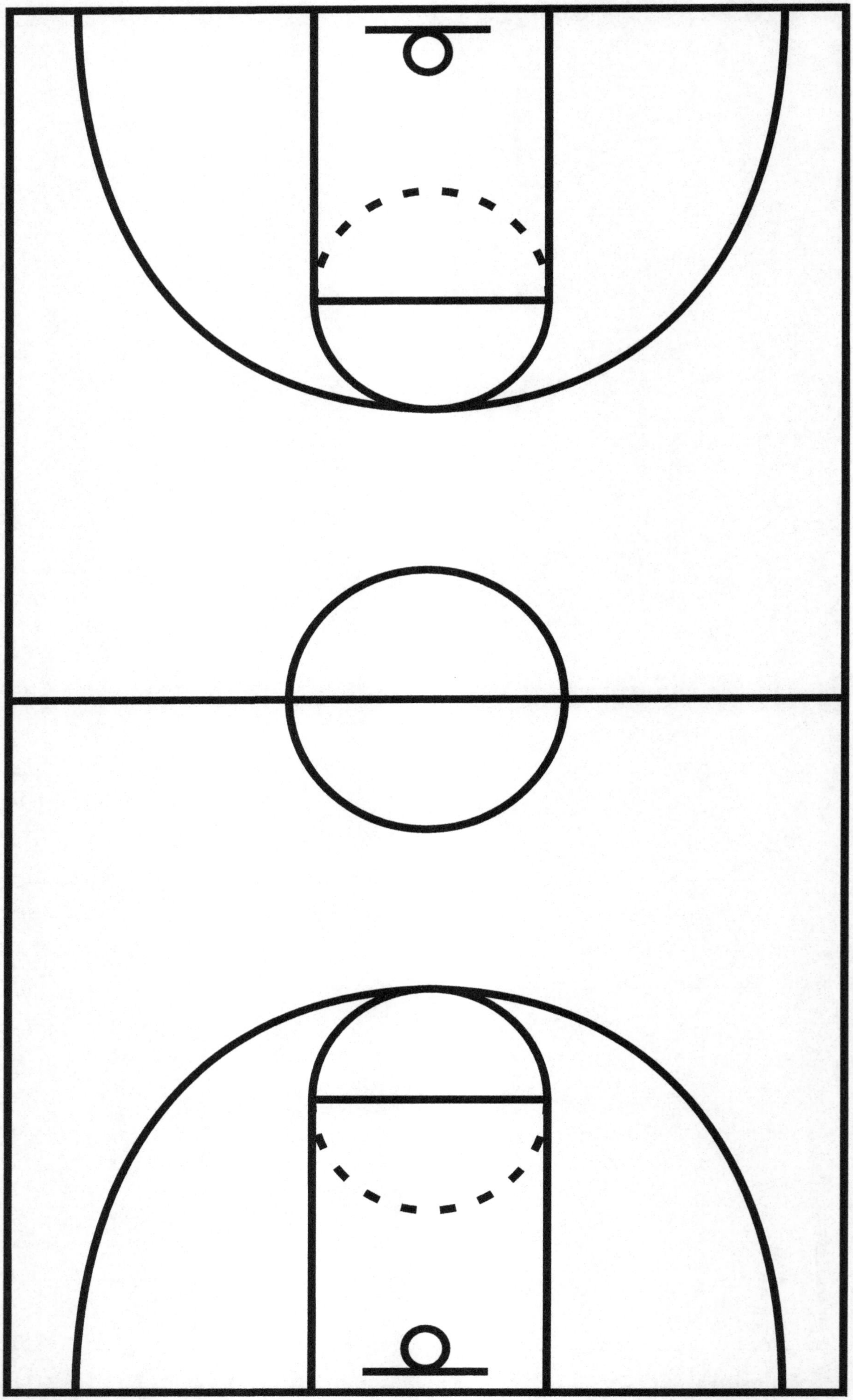

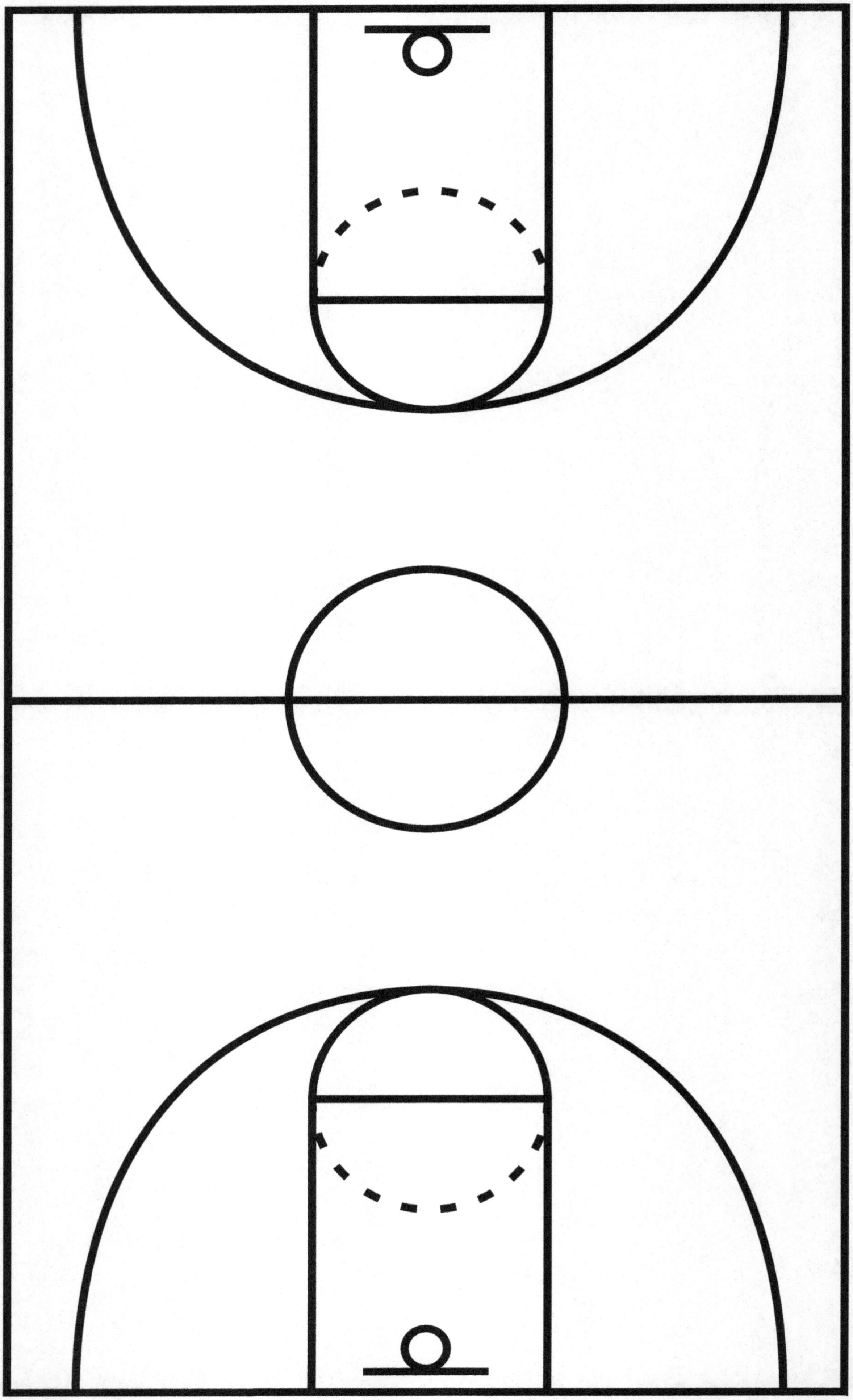

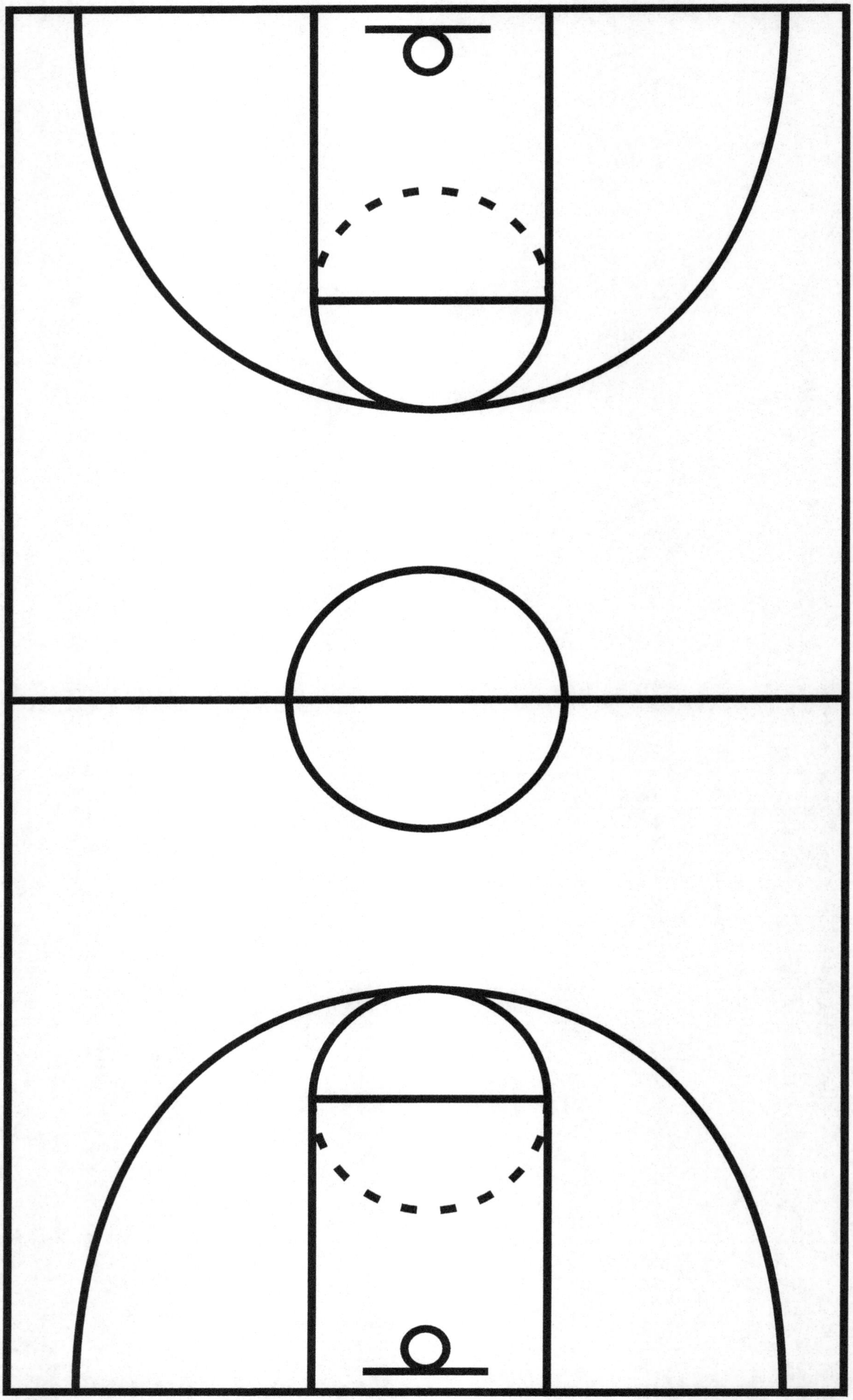

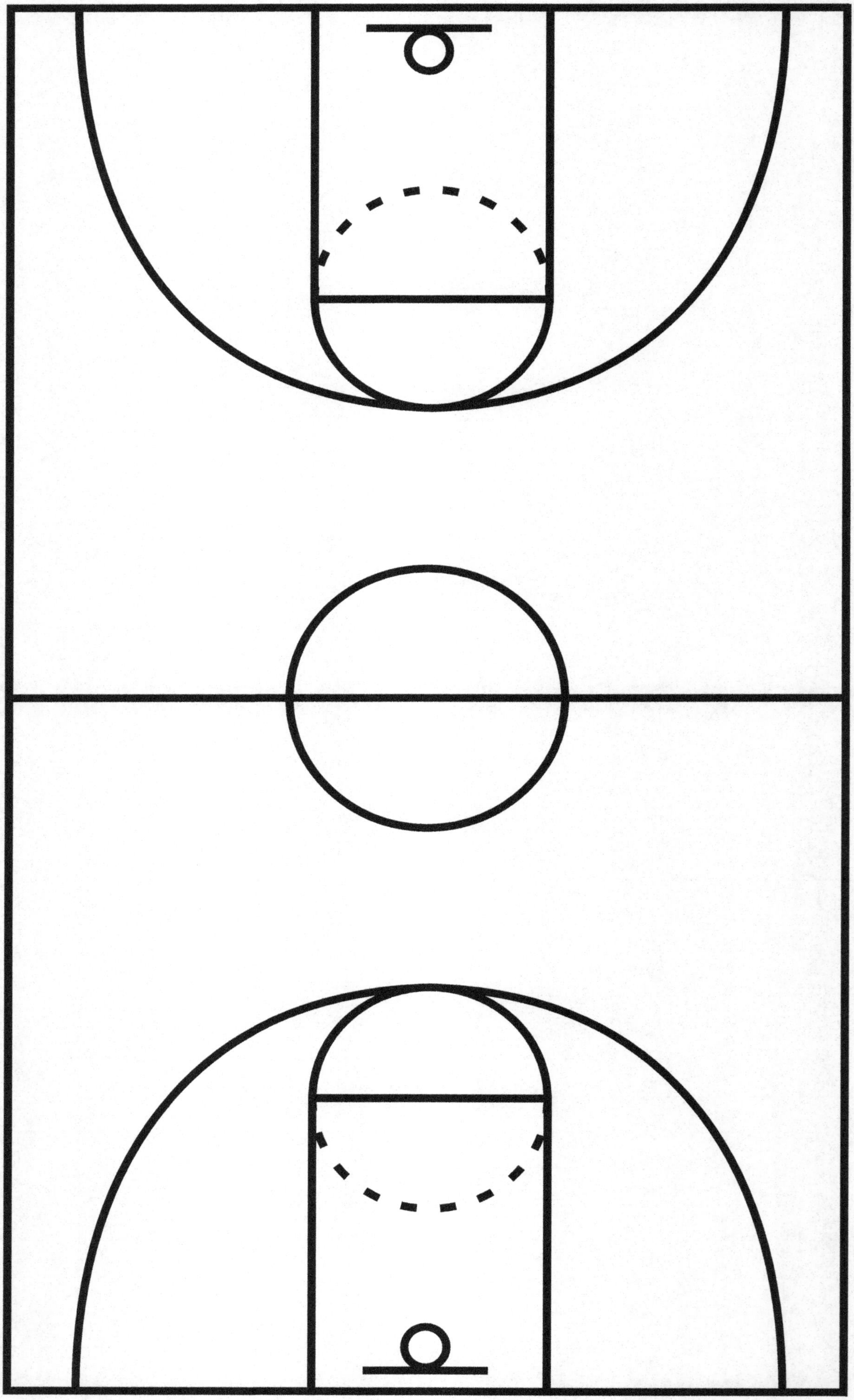

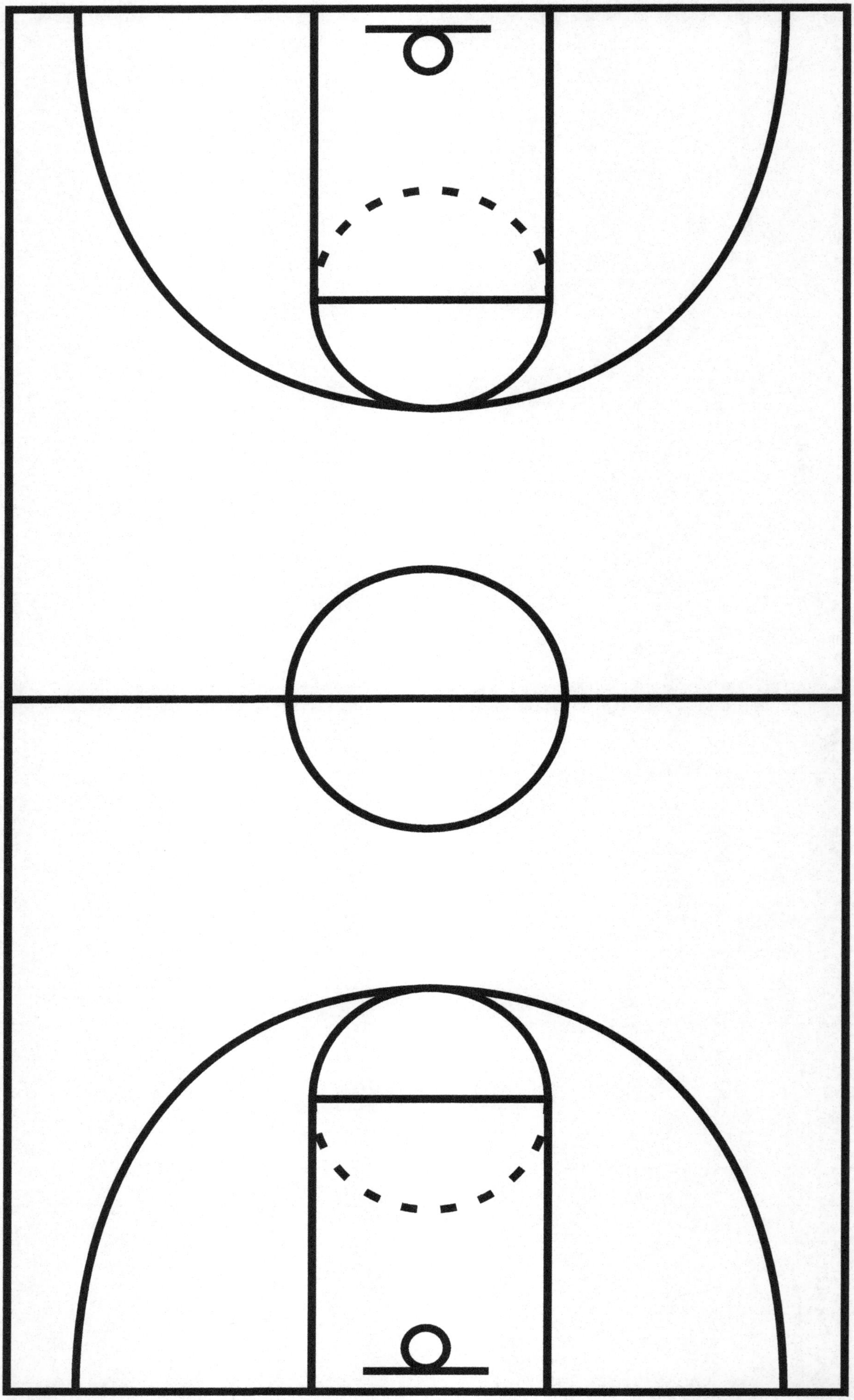

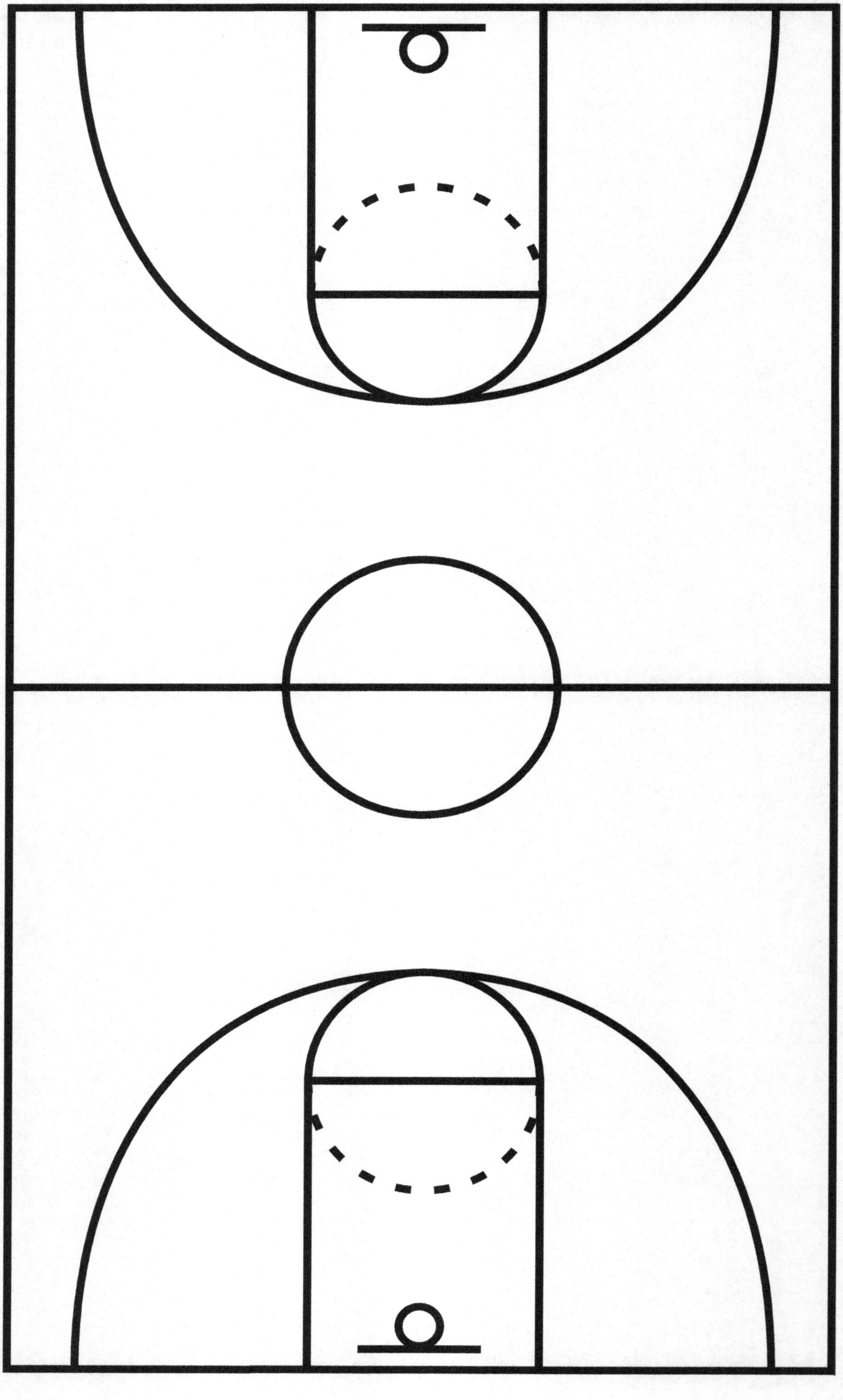

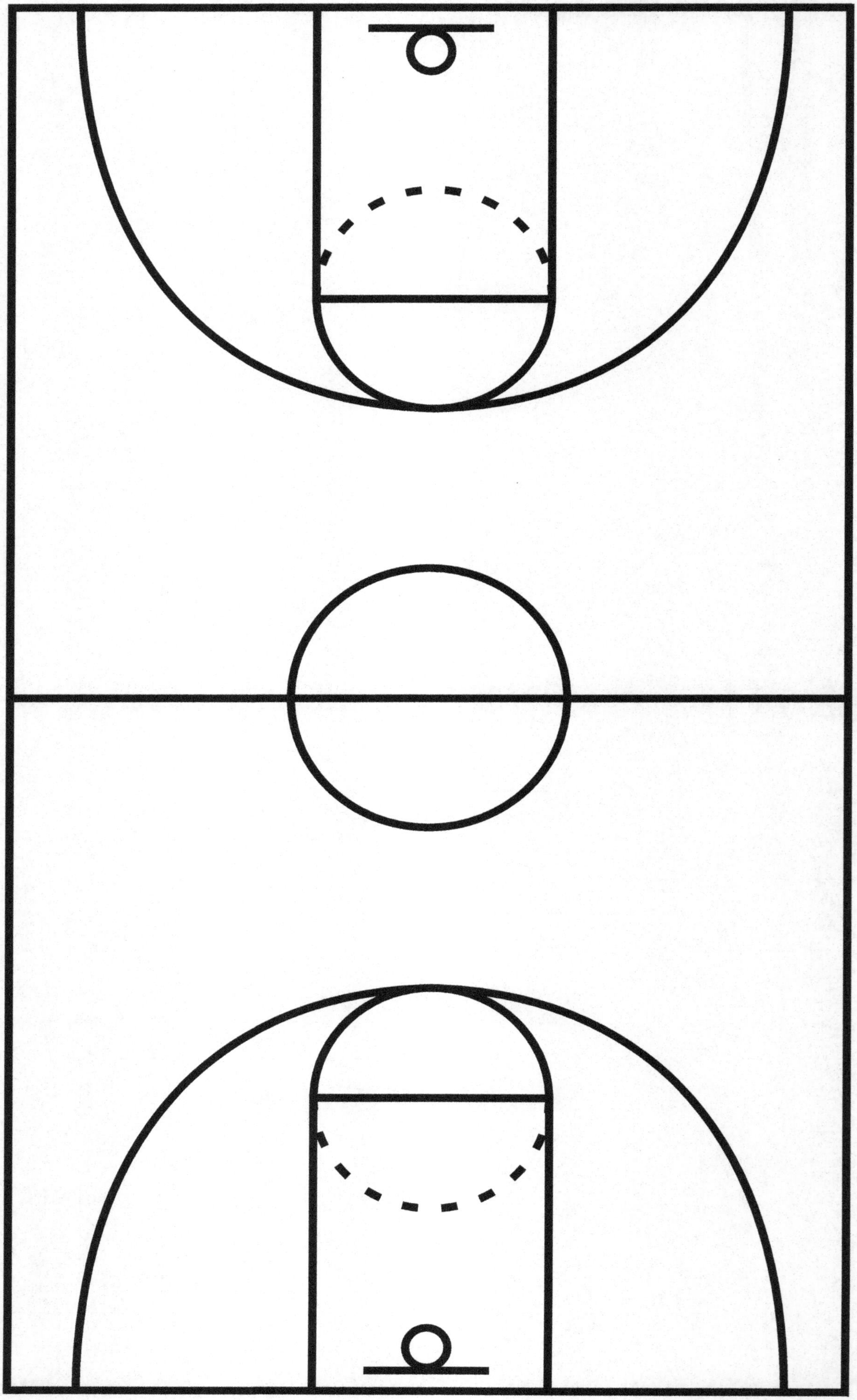

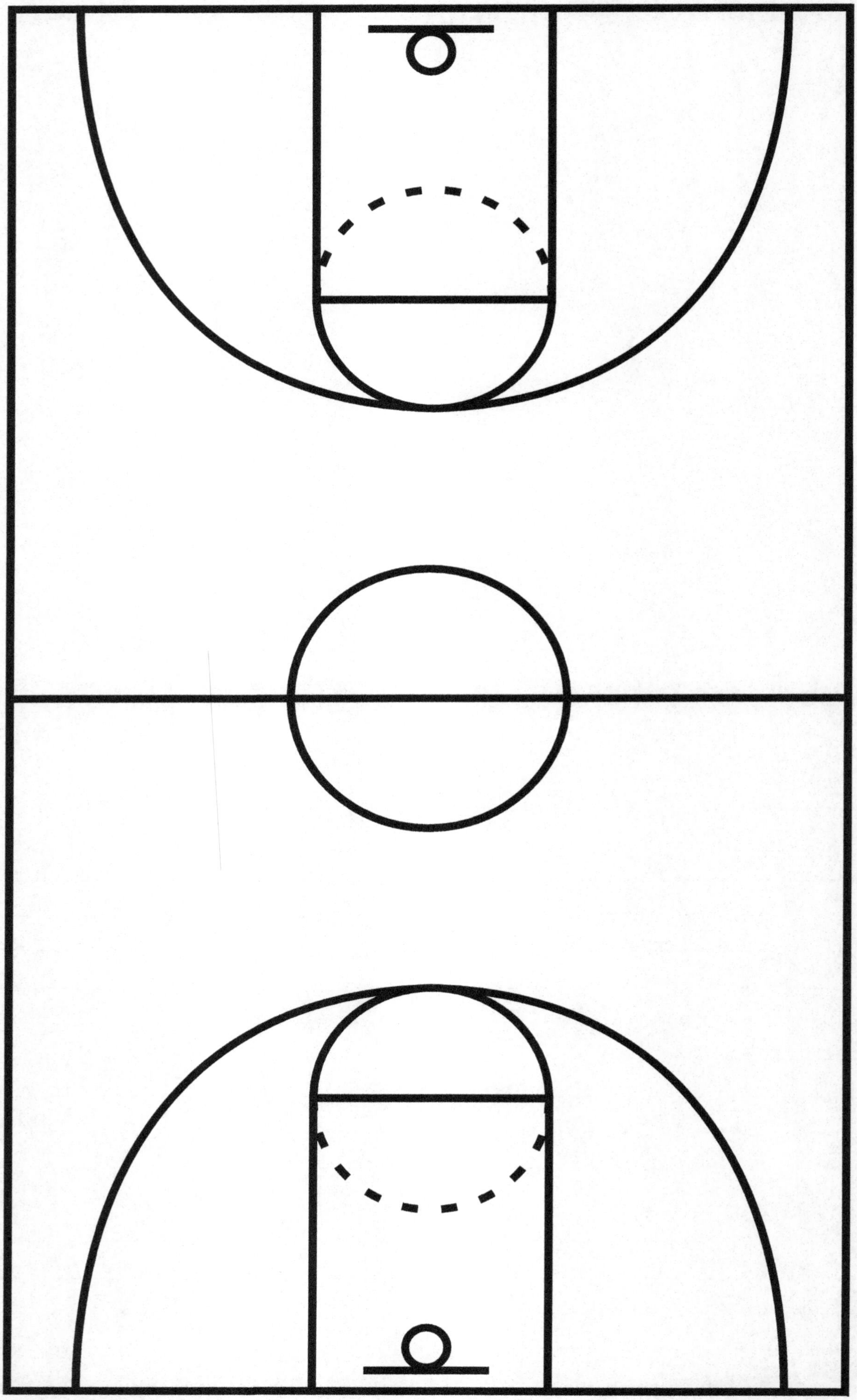

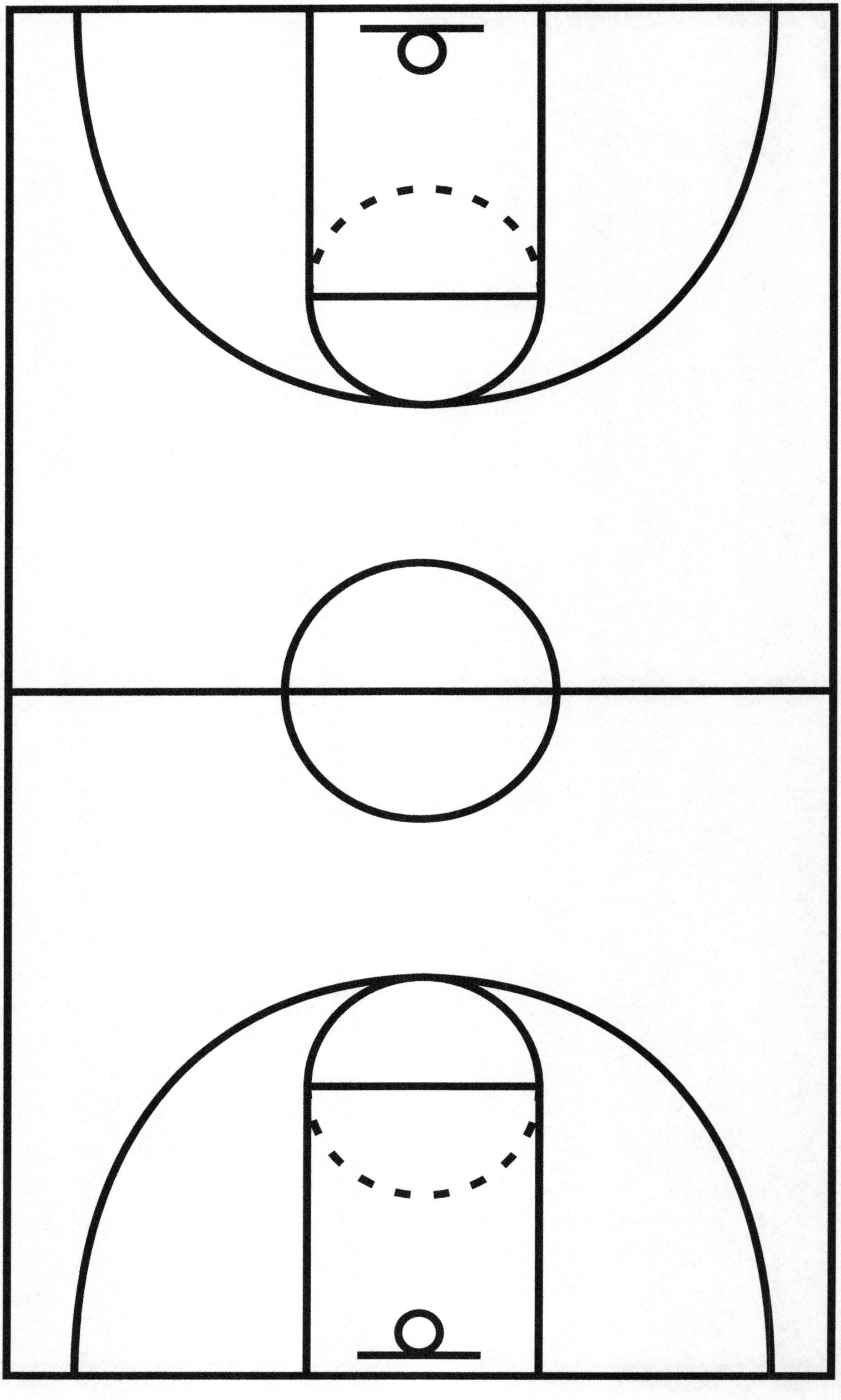

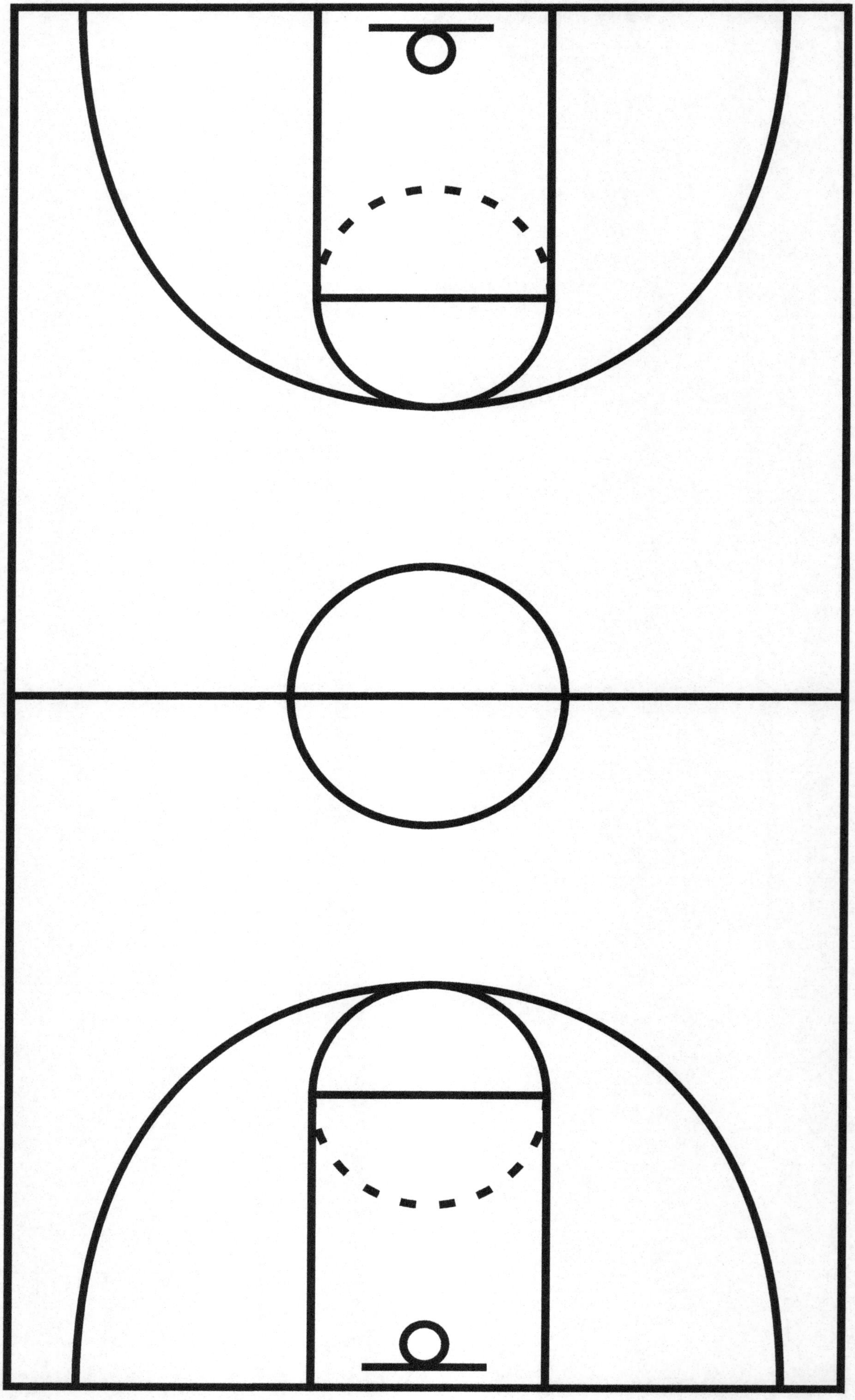

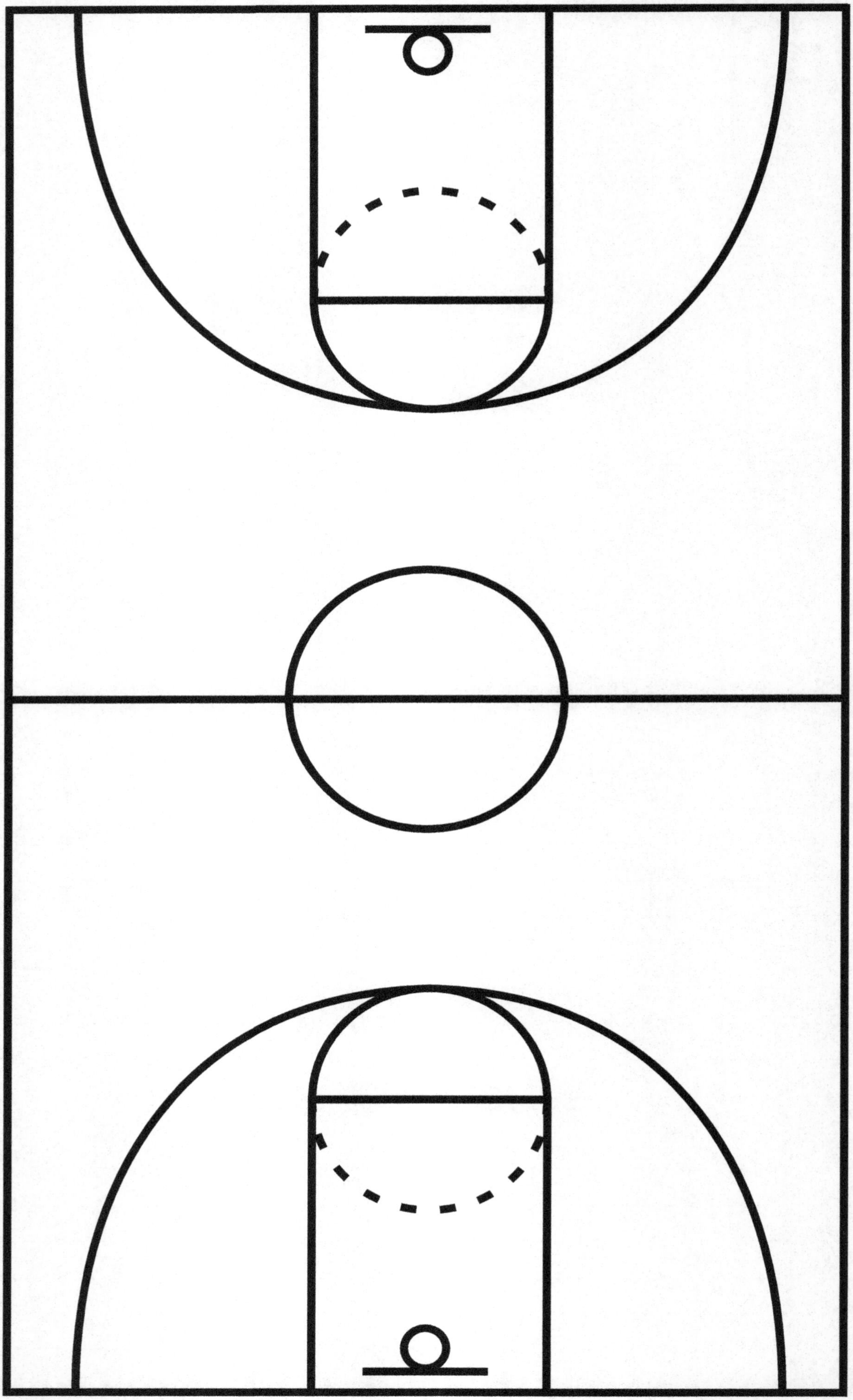

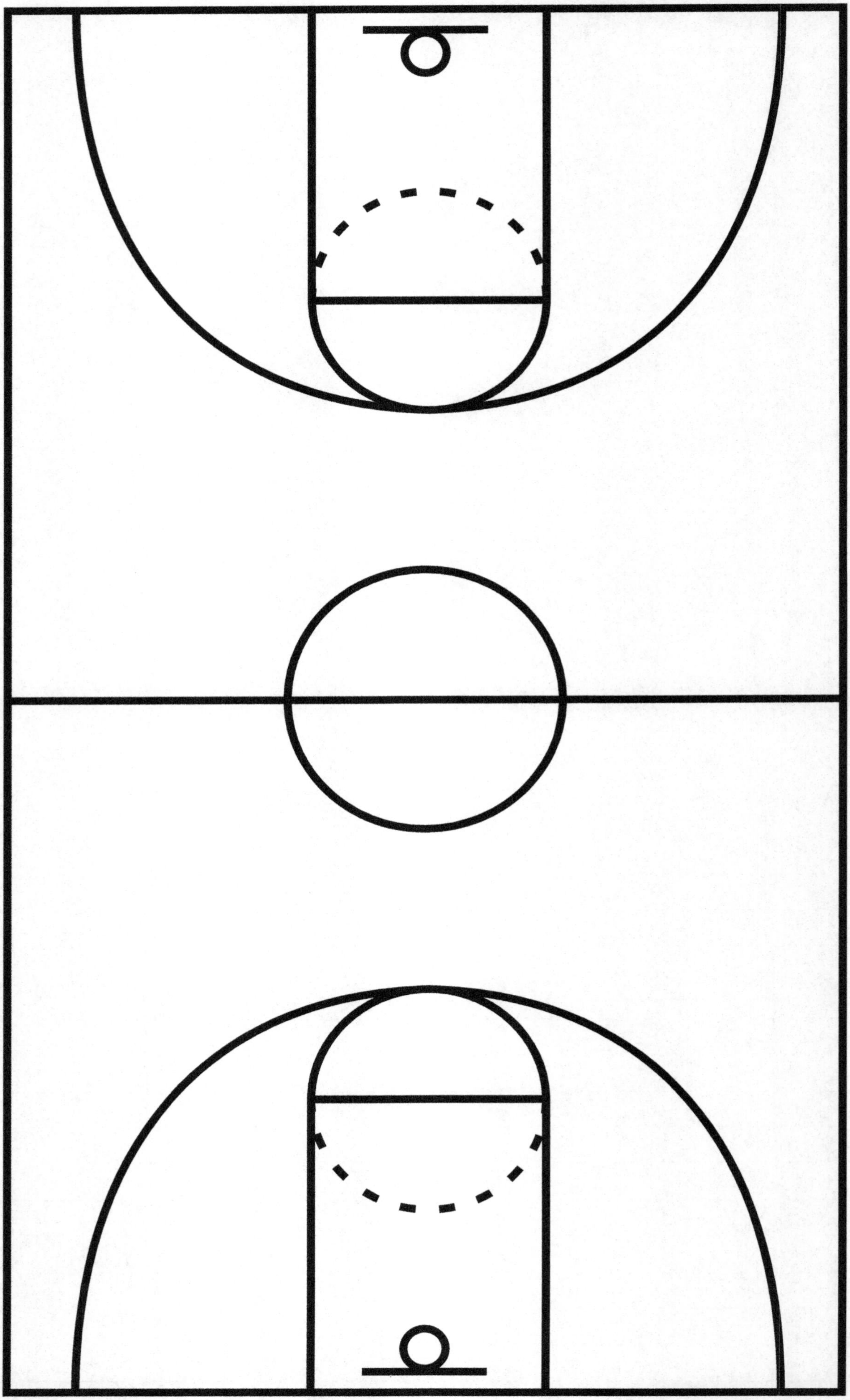

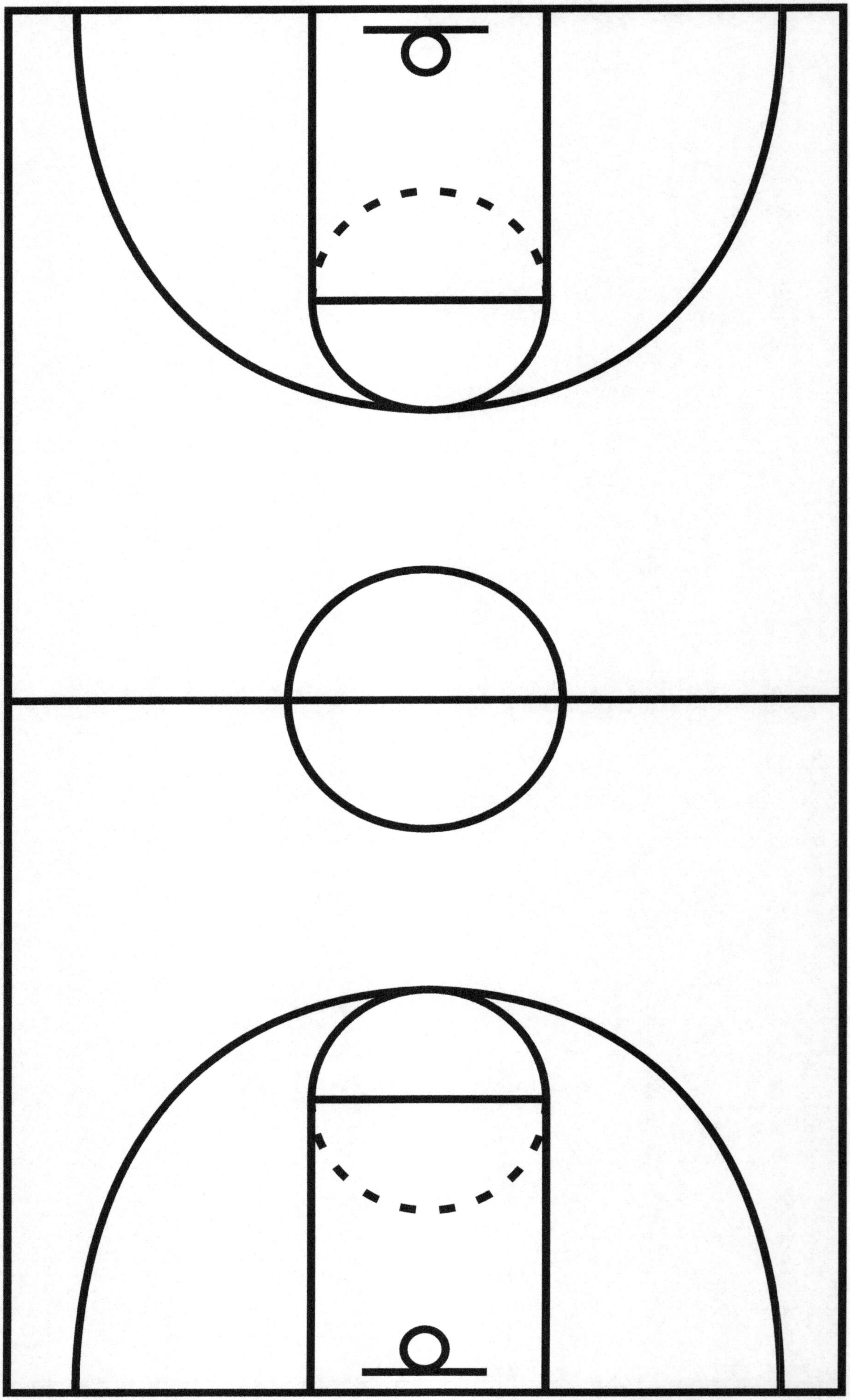

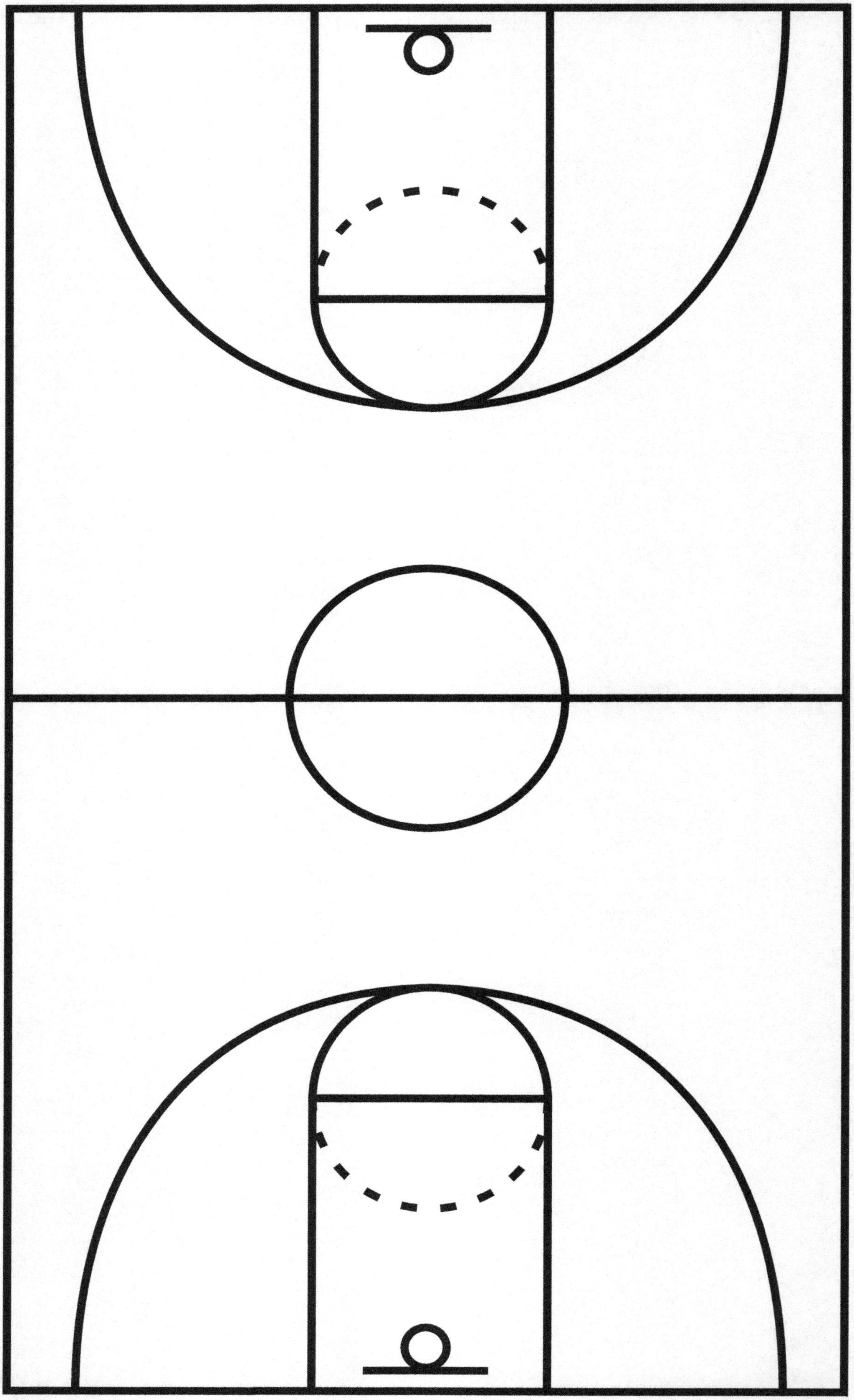

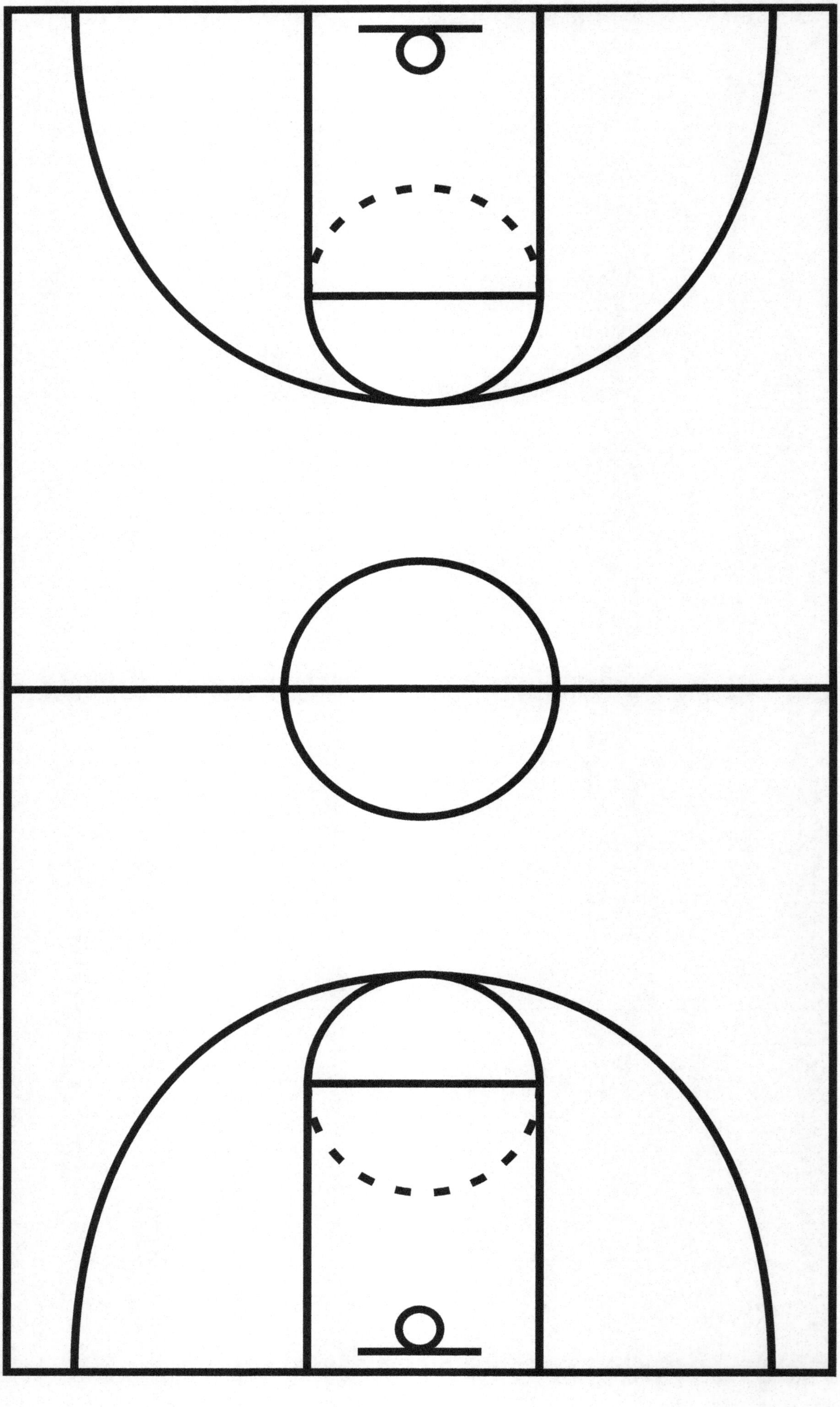

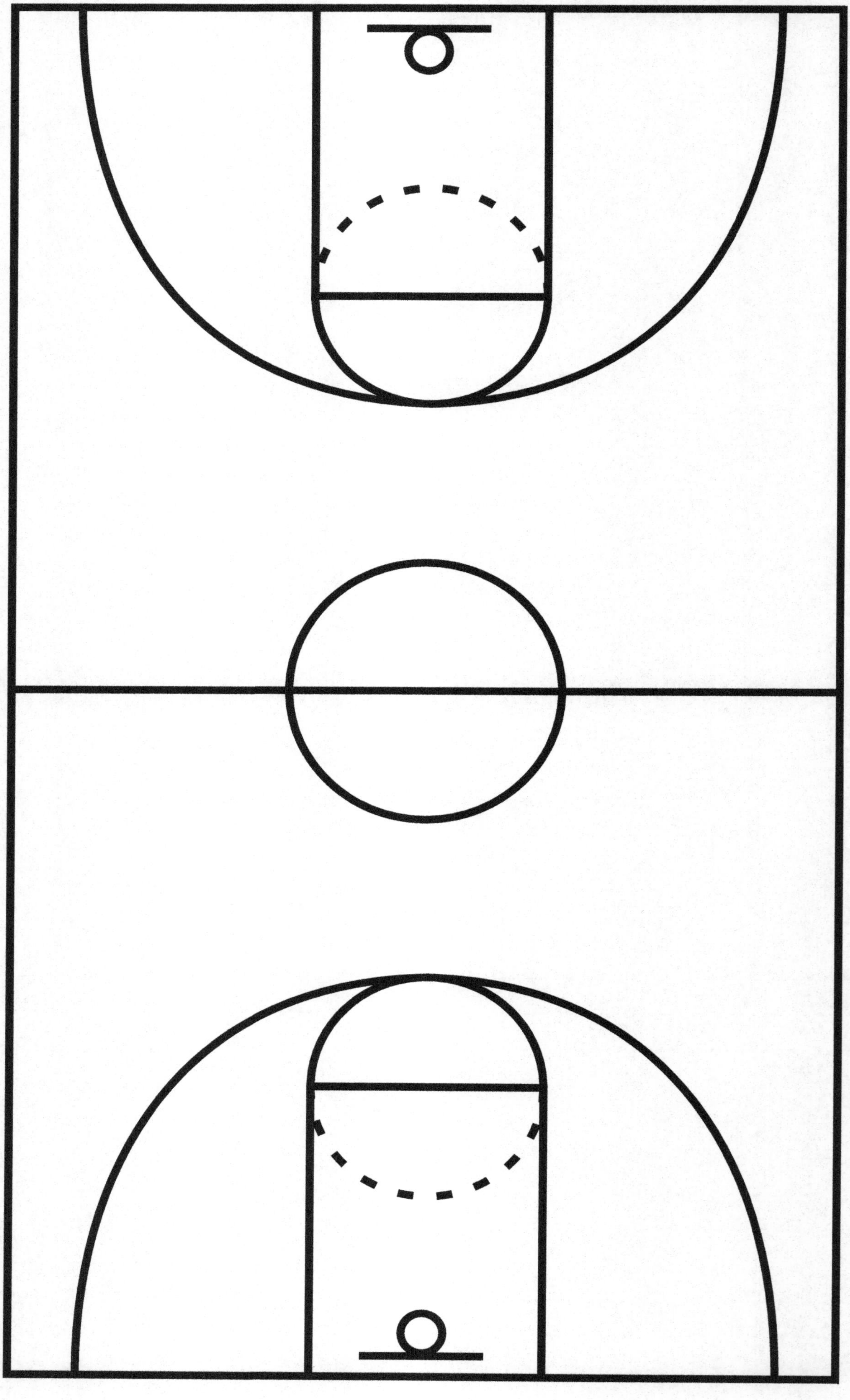

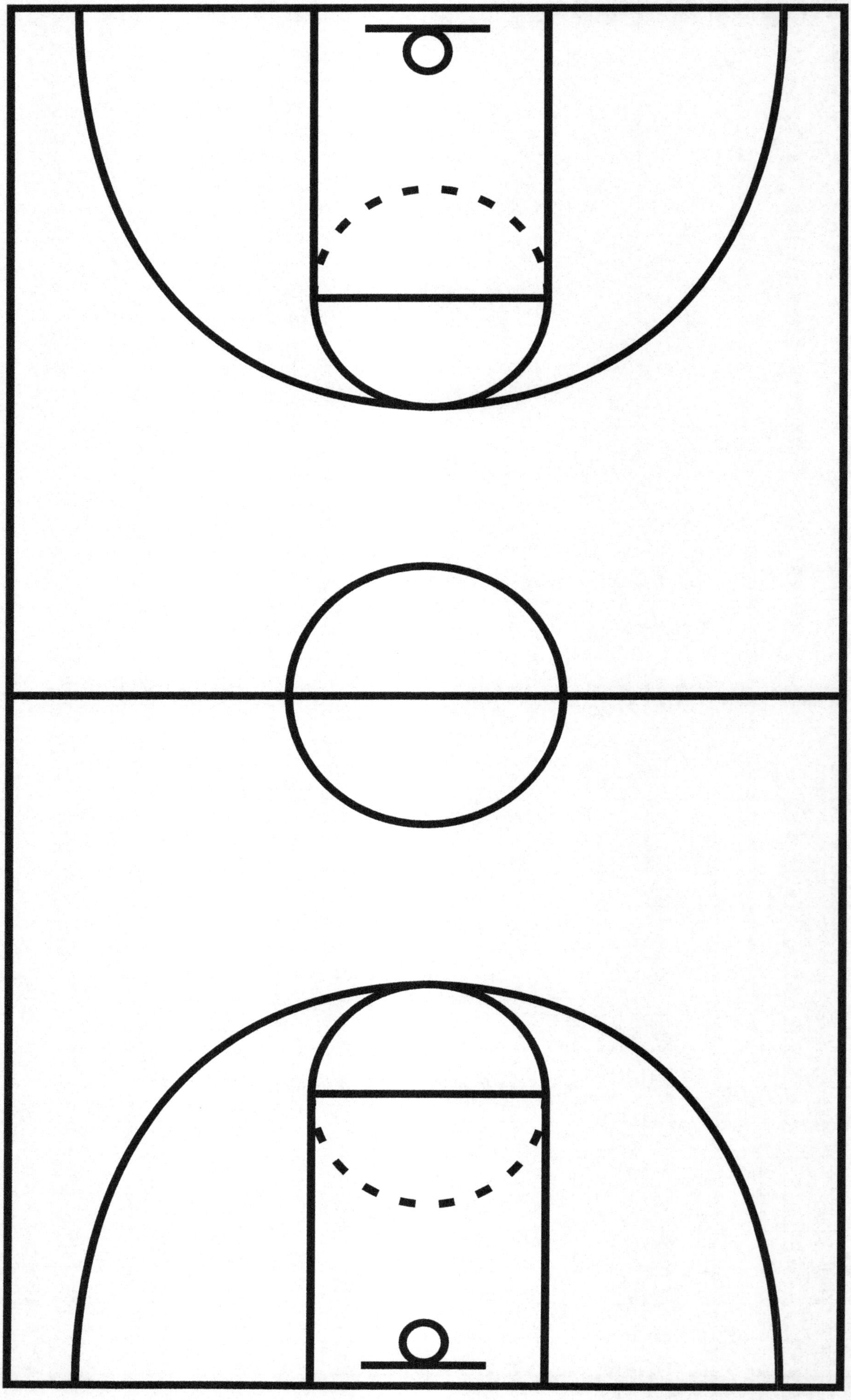

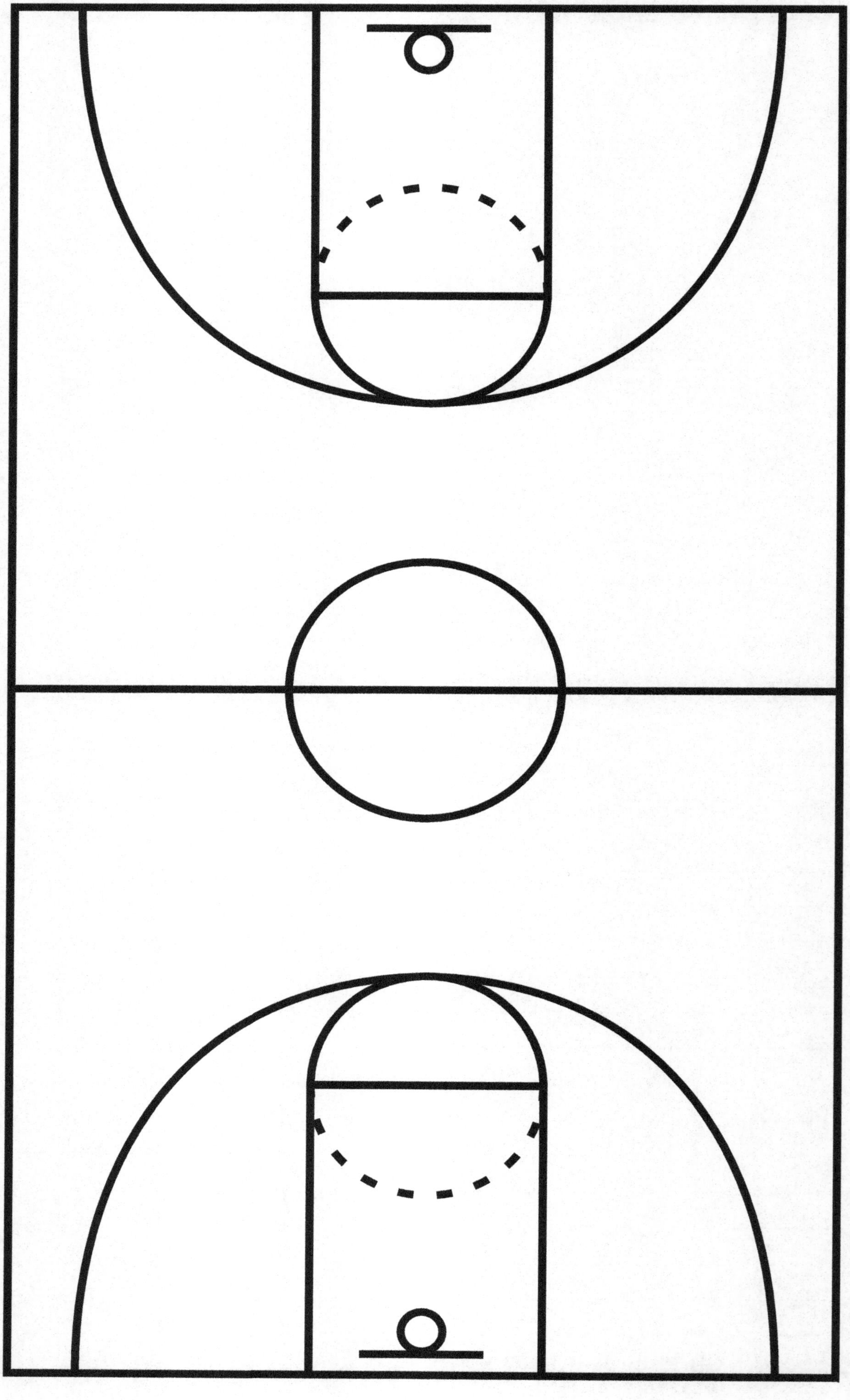

Made in the USA
Monee, IL
20 January 2021

58101667R00083